Challenge Your Child

A Rainbow of Mind-Bending Experiences for the

Fourth Grader

By Becky Daniel

Cover Design
by Terri Moll

Inside Illustrations
by Marty Bucella

Published by Instructional Fair • TS Denison
an imprint of

About the Author

Becky Daniel is a parent, teacher, author, and editor. After graduating from California University at Long Beach, she taught kindergarten through eighth grade. She left the classroom after the birth of her first daughter to care for her child and to pursue a career in writing at home. Now the mother of three, Becky edits a magazine and writes educational books from her home in Orcutt, California. Over the past 25 years, she has written more than 200 educational resource books, including several titles for Instructional Fair • TS Denison.

Credits

Author ....Becky Daniel
Inside Illustrations....................................Marty Bucella
Cover Design...Terri Moll
Cover Photograph ....© Stockbyte
Page and Icon Design...............................Mark Conrad
Project Director ....Kelly Morris Huxmann
Editors ....Kelly Morris Huxmann, Linda Triemstra

McGraw-Hill
Children's Publishing

A Division of The ***McGraw-Hill*** *Companies*

Published by Instructional Fair • TS Denison
An imprint of McGraw-Hill Children's Publishing
Copyright © 2000 McGraw-Hill Children's Publishing

Limited Reproduction Permission: Permission to duplicate these materials is limited to the person for whom they are purchased. Reproduction for an entire school or school district is unlawful and strictly prohibited.

Send all inquiries to:
McGraw-Hill Children's Publishing
3195 Wilson Drive NW
Grand Rapids, Michigan 49544

All Rights Reserved • Printed in the United States of America

Challenge Your Child—Grade 4
ISBN: 0-7424-0041-7

Table of Contents

Introduction

Challenge Your Child is designed to provide a wide range of fun learning experiences for your child. Varied formats tap into all levels of cognition, from basic knowledge to more complex abilities such as comprehension, application, analysis, synthesis, and evaluation. Encourage your child to think on all these levels by recalling, applying, organizing, and assessing learned material.

Take an active role in your child's learning. Guide your child through the activities in this book, focusing on those that are best suited for him or her. Use the activities as a springboard for further investigations. The level of interest you show will serve to increase your child's own motivation.

You will see one very important icon throughout this book. This sign appears on pages that require adult permission, supervision, or other assistance. Be sure your child understands the importance of asking for help in completing these activities.

An answer key is provided in the center of the book for easy self-checking. Simply straighten the staples to remove the pages, then fold the staples again to keep the remainder of the book intact.

Who Ordered Pizza?

Three friends went to a restaurant for lunch. Read the facts and fill in the chart to discover who had pizza, who had a burger, and who had chicken.

Facts:

1. The girl ate either a burger or chicken.
2. Either Jason ate a burger and Alice had chicken or Alice ate a burger and Jason had pizza.
3. Marco ate either a burger or pizza.

	pizza	burger	chicken
Alice			
Jason			
Marco			

analysis

Word Associations

Cross out the word in each row that does not belong.

1. discus	football	basketball	gumball
2. boot	sandal	sock	clog
3. camera	watch	calendar	clock
4. hand	foot	head	hat
5. lemon	cherry	orange	grapefruit
6. bicycle	buggy	jeep	bed
7. glasses	window	windshield	toupee
8. surgeon	dentist	lawyer	veterinarian
9. backpack	book	bucket	purse
10. microwave	toaster	refrigerator	teakettle

© Instructional Fair • TS Denison

Anagram Zoo

An *anagram* is a word that is spelled by rearranging the letters of another word. How many animals and their anagrams can you list?

8-10 Amateur **11-15 Ace** **16-20 Genius**

Example: cat act

1. __________ __________
2. __________ __________
3. __________ __________
4. __________ __________
5. __________ __________
6. __________ __________
7. __________ __________
8. __________ __________
9. __________ __________
10. __________ __________
11. __________ __________
12. __________ __________
13. __________ __________
14. __________ __________
15. __________ __________
16. __________ __________
17. __________ __________
18. __________ __________
19. __________ __________
20. __________ __________

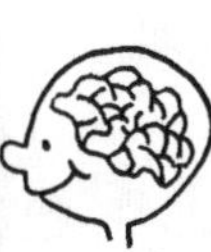

Brain Booster: Write a short sentence. Try to use every letter in the sentence to write a new sentence.

© Instructional Fair • TS Denison

Rebus Ending

Decode the rebus to read the final words from a famous children's book.

"  – p  – p in a

c +  – g b +  herself.

 – m is  of + 10

t +  some + 1  – r

along 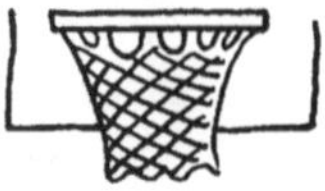 – p is a

true f +  + nd – c &

a g +  – w wr +  + er.

– i + lotte  – p both."

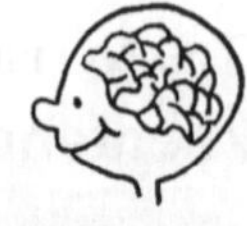

Brain Booster: Name the children's book that ends with this quote.

© Instructional Fair • TS Denison

Who Owns Which Pet?

Luis, Hannah, Martin, and Kathy each have a different pet (dachshund, cat, frog, and parrot). Read the facts to find out which pet belongs to which child. Draw a line from each child to the correct pet.

Facts:

1. The girl with long hair has a pet that cannot hop or fly.
2. The dachshund belongs to one of the boys.
3. The frog belongs to a girl.
4. Martin's pet cannot talk.

Luis 

Hannah 

Martin 

Kathy 

Brain Booster: Write four new clues that will match each pet owner with a different pet.

© Instructional Fair • TS Denison

Relating

Complete each analogy with an appropriate word.
Example: **sock** is to **foot** as **glove** is to **hand**.

1. **Cup** is to **adult** as **bottle** is to ____________________
2. **Four** is to **dog** as **two** is to ____________________
3. **Skin** is to **human** as **feathers** are to ____________________
4. **Paw** is to **dog** as **hoof** is to ____________________
5. **Hot** is to **oven** as **cold** is to ____________________
6. **Watch** is to **wrist** as **ring** is to ____________________
7. **Round** is to **ball** as **square** is to ____________________
8. **Calf** is to **cow** as **foal** is to ____________________
9. **Antlers** are to **deer** as **horns** are to ____________________
10. **Ink** is to **pen** as **paint** is to ____________________
11. **Rain** is to **spring** as **snow** is to ____________________
12. **Tadpole** is to **frog** as **caterpillar** is to ____________________

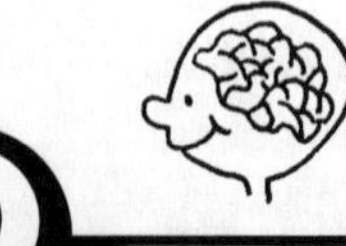

Brain Booster: Make up your own analogies.

© Instructional Fair • TS Denison

Write It Like It Is!

Can you write a word or phrase in a way that convey its meaning? Try with the words and phrases below.

G E S G = scrambled eggs

high chair

downtown

circle of friends

understanding mom

square dancing

uptight

Brain Booster: Come up with your own words and phrases to write in a special way. Show them to family and friends. Can they guess the answers?

© Instructional Fair • TS Denison

Colorful Feelings

If you could see feelings in color, what would they look like? Color each feeling below.

impatience

anger

joy worry

pride fear

loneliness

sadness

Phonics Code

Some combinations of letters and numbers can sound like whole words. Example: GR8 = great. Write the word suggested by each set of letters and numbers below.

1. B4 ________________
2. A4D ________________
3. 2TH ________________
4. YY ________________
5. B8 ________________
6. APP ________________
7. FRII ________________
8. 1DER ________________
9. CCND ________________
10. PL8 ________________
11. B& ________________
12. EE ________________
13. XL ________________
14. ST8 ________________
15. 4M ________________
16. AQQ ________________
17. D88 ________________
18. TP ________________

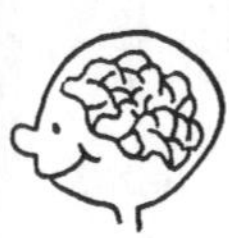

Brain Booster: Decipher this sentence: B4UAQQJ?. Write two sentences using a mix of letters and numbers.

________________ ________________

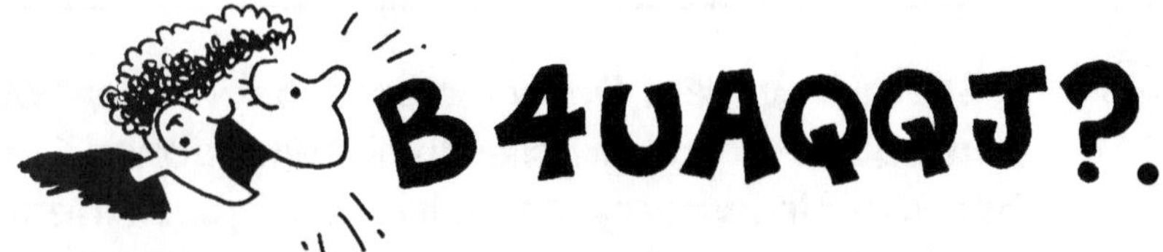

© Instructional Fair • TS Denison

Compound Fun

A compound word is made up of two or more smaller words. Example: **fireplace** = **fire** + **place**. Can you think of a compound word for each picture below?

1. 

____

5. 

____

2. 

____

6. 

____

3. 

____

7. 

____

4. 

____

8. 

____

Brain Booster: Draw pictures to represent other compound words, such as fishbowl, bookend, letter-head, or strawberry. Ask a friend to guess the words.

© Instructional Fair • TS Denison

Car Search

How many car dealerships are in your area? To find out, look in the yellow pages. Answer the questions below as you conduct your search.

1. Under what heading are car dealerships listed? ________________
2. How many different makes of cars are listed? __________
   Choose ten. List them alphabetically in the chart below.
3. Tally the total number of dealerships that sell each make of car.
4. Which make has the most dealerships in your area?________
   Which make has the fewest?__________
5. For each make, list the phone number of the dealership nearest you.

Make of Car	Total Number of Dealerships	Phone Number of Dealership Nearest You

Brain Booster: Can you find a place near you that rents stretch limousines? What is the name of the company?

____

© Instructional Fair • TS Denison

Following Directions

Follow the directions to draw a picture in the box.

1. Draw a road along the bottom of the picture.
2. Draw a side view of a car on the road near the bottom right corner.
3. Give the car windows and a front and back door.
4. In the upper left-hand corner, draw a half moon.
5. In the upper right-hand corner, draw six big stars.
6. In the lower left-hand corner, draw people walking beside the road
7. Color the car a color that rhymes with *spread*.
8. Color the sky a color that rhymes with *shellac*.
9. Color the road a color that rhymes with *weigh*.

Brain Booster: Write ten directions to draw a picture. Give the directions to a friend. How does your friend's finished picture look?

© Instructional Fair • TS Denison

Perfect Personification

synthesis

Personification means giving animals or inanimate objects human qualities or characteristics. Example: The smiling moon looked down on me. Illustrate each example of personification below.

The flag waved at me.

The ringing bell pierced the air.

The leaves skipped across the yard.

The warm sun massaged my back.

The storm shook me awake.

Thoughts carried me home.

Brain Booster: On another sheet of paper, write a sentence or two using personification. Draw pictures to illustrate your sentences.

© Instructional Fair • TS Denison

Paradise

Imagine that you and your best friend must live on a deserted island for one year. The water on the island is safe to drink, and fish are plentiful. Ten crops grow abundantly on the island. Find them in the puzzle below.

T	C	T	O	M	I	D	H	J	E	N	A	X	O	K	I	S
O	P	A	X	R	Y	L	C	A	S	H	E	W	S	R	T	N
M	T	P	I	N	E	A	P	P	L	E	S	P	A	Y	Q	U
A	N	D	C	F	B	V	N	N	K	G	Y	A	M	N	S	S
T	B	K	H	E	Y	C	I	C	T	H	E	P	G	B	T	E
O	E	O	R	A	N	G	E	S	L	D	R	A	E	C	O	R
E	A	M	J	N	D	C	O	R	N	O	R	Y	O	R	N	I
S	N	P	F	J	H	T	M	U	S	P	S	A	L	S	D	C
V	S	O	G	E	A	B	A	N	A	N	A	S	A	I	U	E
C	A	V	O	C	A	D	O	E	S	I	N	G	O	P	C	Z

There is no electricity on the island, but it is warm year-round. List additional supplies you will need. You may select ten items.

1. ______________________
2. ______________________
3. ______________________
4. ______________________
5. ______________________
6. ______________________
7. ______________________
8. ______________________
9. ______________________
10. ______________________

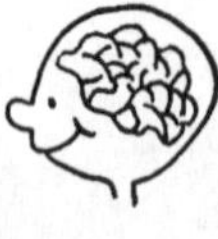

Brain Booster: Draw a picture of the island. Indicate where everything is and places where you would build or store your things.

© Instructional Fair • TS Denison

The Pet Parade at School

How good is your memory? Read the story several times. Then answer as many of the questions on page 20 as you can without looking back at the story.

Amy ambled along with an armload of ants.
Bob and his bullfrog Boomerang danced.
Carlos gave his cute calico cat Candy a ride.
Dagmar daintily dangled a colorful dragonfly.
Eric escorted an enormous earthbound emu.
Flo's fat, flapping, flamboyant flamingo flew.
Gertrude and goose got off a green and gold bus,
Hidden behind Harry and his high-stepping hippopotamus.
Iggy's iguana inched along leaving an icky track.
Jeremy's jerboa joyfully jumped from his backpack.
Katy was carried by Kanga, a kangaroo mama.
Larry lassoed Lucy, a long-legged, lopsided llama.
Maurice masterfully maneuvered a monster moose.
Nancy's naughty nag named Nanette got loose.
Olga organized Oscar, an ornery old octopus.
Priscilla paraded Pedro, a flat-as-dust platypus.
Quentin couldn't quiet his quirky, quacking quetzal bird.
The racket stampeded **R**alph's racing rhino herd.
Sam's hissy snake slithered between two blue cans,
And scared the **T**wang twins' two trained toucans.
Ulysses rode under an umbrella on a unicorn's horn.
Vera's vintage vulture just gazed forlorn.
Wesley wrestled his walloping walrus into a box.
Xavier exercised Tex, an extraordinary red fox.
Yolanda yelled at a young, yelping, yellow yak.
But the best zoomed in last, on a zebra's back.
It was **Z**igfried and his zig-zagging, zippy zebu
Who won first prize in the parade at school.

© Instructional Fair • TS Denison

More Pet Parade

Now that you've read "The Pet Parade at School," try to answer the questions below.

1. Who rode in on a zebra's back? ____________________
2. The Twang twins brought two trained ____________________.
3. What was the name of the ornery old octopus that Olga brought? ____________________
4. What shape was Priscilla's platypus named Pedro? ____________________
5. What pet did Katy bring to school? ____________________
6. What did Iggy's iguana do? ____________________
7. What did Flo's fat, flapping, flamboyant flamingo do? ____________________
8. Eric escorted an enormous earthbound pet. What was it? ____________________
9. What was right ahead of Iggy's iguana? ____________________
10. Who had a racing rhino herd? ____________________

Just for Fun: Find the percentage of questions you answered correctly. Each correct answer is worth 10%.

Say It with a Simile

A *simile* describes something by comparing it to something else. Draw a line from each adjective to the correct phrase to create twelve animal similes.

slow	as a bee
big	as a lamb
happy	as a fox
silly	as an ant
hardworking	as a lark
stubborn	as a turtle
wise	as a moose
gentle	as an owl
fierce	as a peacock
proud	as a tiger
busy	as a mule
sly	as a goose

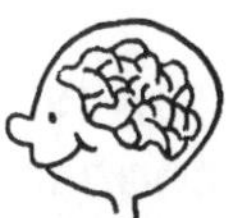

Brain Booster: Illustrate one or more of the similes you've created. Then try writing your own.

A to Z Names

Can you think of names that begin with each letter of the alphabet? Write one boy's name and one girl's name for each letter.

A ______________________

B ______________________

C ______________________

D ______________________

E ______________________

F ______________________

G ______________________

H ______________________

I ______________________

J ______________________

K ______________________

L ______________________

M ______________________

N ______________________

O ______________________

P ______________________

Q ______________________

R ______________________

S ______________________

T ______________________

U ______________________

V ______________________

W ______________________

X ______________________

Y ______________________

Z ______________________

Brain Booster: Make other A to Z lists of animals, foods, cities, song titles,or anything else you choose.

© Instructional Fair • TS Denison

Homonym Help

Homonyms are words that are pronounced the same but spelled differently. Examples: to, two, and too. Find the homonyms that have been used incorrectly in the story below. Then rewrite the story correctly.

Four to weaks eye have Ben baking cakes with read icing. Ewe can knot waist flower and sugar, sew eye eight every won of the cakes. Of coarse, my waste is getting bigger. Eye am getting as big as a hoarse. The plane fact is, I blue my diet.

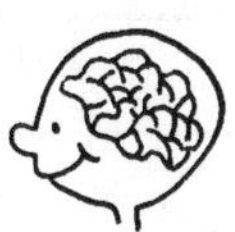

Brain Booster: Make a list of at least ten more homonym pairs. Use them in a short story.

© Instructional Fair • TS Denison

analysis

Onomatopoetry

Onomatopoeia is creating words based on sounds. Tweet, croak, crash, and boom are just a few examples.

Match each sound word with its source. Write the letter on the blank.

(a) (b) (c) (d) (e) (f)

____ hiss ____ pop ____ whine

____ howl ____ sizzle ____ whir

Describe two possible sources for each sound.

1. honk ____________________ ____________________
2. thump ____________________ ____________________
3. buzz ____________________ ____________________
4. snap ____________________ ____________________

Write a poem using onomatopoetic words.

____

____

____

____

____

____

© Instructional Fair • TS Denison

Line Design

Create a line design. Write a number at each point on the circle. Then use a ruler to draw lines between each pair of like numbers. Color your finished design.

Example: 1 3 1 2 1

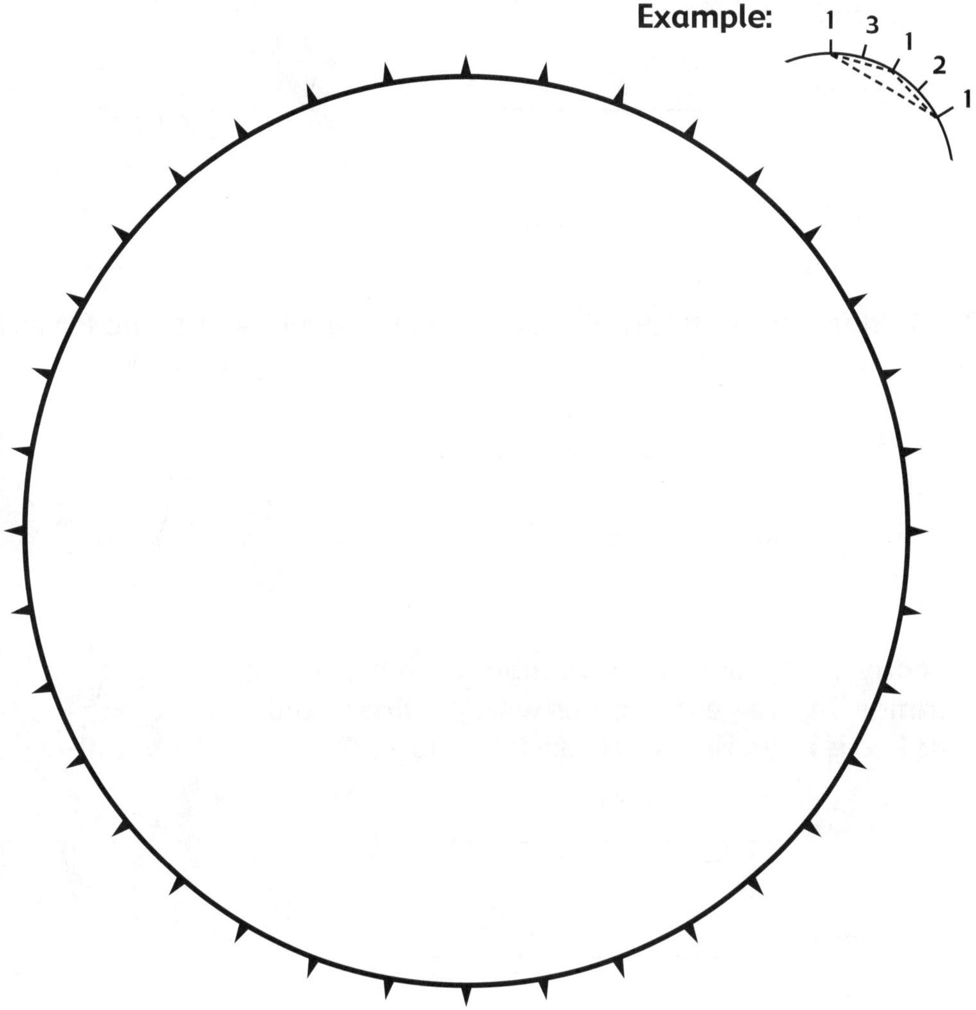

Just for Fun: Create more line designs using different number patterns.

© Instructional Fair • TS Denison

How Old?

analysis

Use the facts to determine each person's age.

1. Today Javier is three times as old as his sister Luisa. In two years he will only be twice as old as his sister. How old are Javier and Luisa today?

Javier ______________________

Luisa ______________________

2. A father is three times his son's age. In twenty years, the father will be only twice as old as his son. How old are they today?

father ______________________

son ______________________

3. Today Leo is four years younger than his brother James. In five years, James will be twice as old as Leo is now. How old is each boy today?

Leo ______________________

James ______________________

Brain Booster: Abby has two older sisters. The sum of the three sisters' ages is twenty. How can this be true if one sister is six and the other is eight?

© Instructional Fair • TS Denison

Coordinate It

Follow the directions to discover the secret picture.

Plot each point and label with the correct number.

1 (A, 7)	4 (D, 5)	7 (L, 8)	10 (L, 11)	13 (H, 9)
2 (C, 5)	5 (J, 7)	8 (O, 10)	11 (J, 10)	14 (D, 6)
3 (C, 3)	6 (K, 6)	9 (P, 12)	12 (F, 11)	15 (A, 7)

Connect the points in order from 1 to 15.

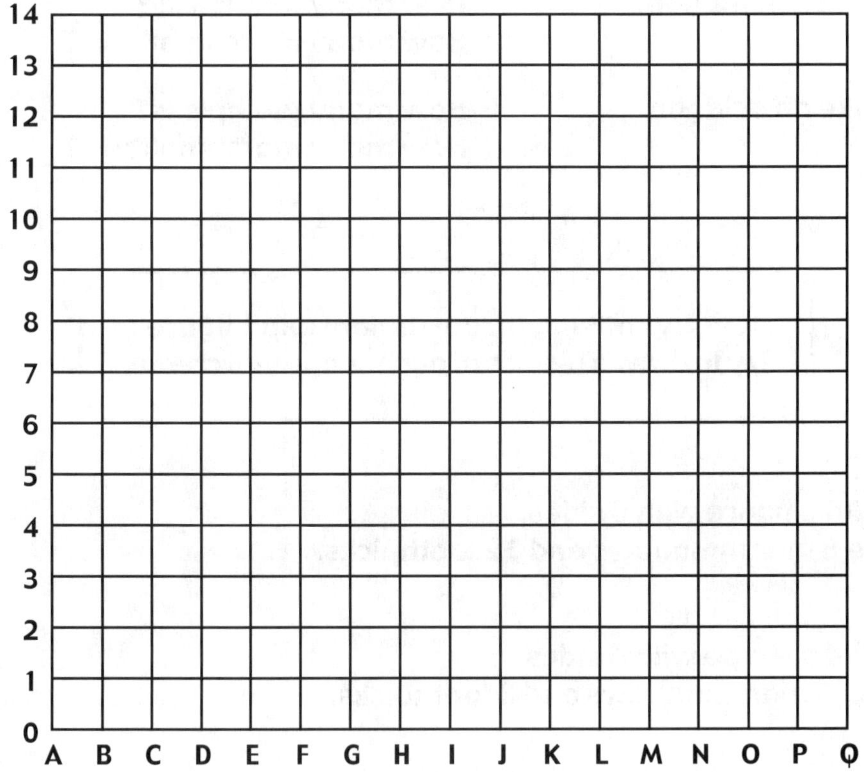

14 13 12 11 10 9 8 7 6 5 4 3 2 1 0

A B C D E F G H I J K L M N O P Q

Brain Booster: Make your own pictures and designs by plotting points on graph paper or a hand-drawn grid.

© Instructional Fair • TS Denison

The Shape of Things

Make models of geometric shapes using toothpicks and miniature marshmallows. Draw each shape.

1. Make a triangle. How many toothpicks? ____ How many marshmallows? ____

2. Make a diamond. How many toothpicks? ____ How many marshmallows? ____

3. Make a pentagon. How many toothpicks? ____ How many marshmallows? ____

4. Make an octagon. How many toothpicks? ____ How many marshmallows? ____

Now try making three-dimensional figures. Try to draw a picture of each shape you create.

5. Build a figure with 6 sides. Use 8 marshmallows and 12 toothpicks.

6. Build a shape with 4 sides. Use 5 marshmallows and 8 toothpicks.

Brain Booster: Can you build a solid using a pentagon for each side? How many marshmallows do you need? How many toothpicks do you need?

© Instructional Fair • TS Denison

Star Connection

Arrange nine stars in such a way that you can draw ten straight lines with exactly three stars in each line.

★ ★ ★ ★ ★ ★ ★ ★ ★

Use scratch paper to practice. Then draw your final answer in the box below.

Brain Booster: Make up your own star and line challenge for a friend.

It All Adds Up!

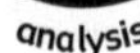

Arrange the numerals 1 through 9 in the circles so that the sum of each line of three circles equals 18.

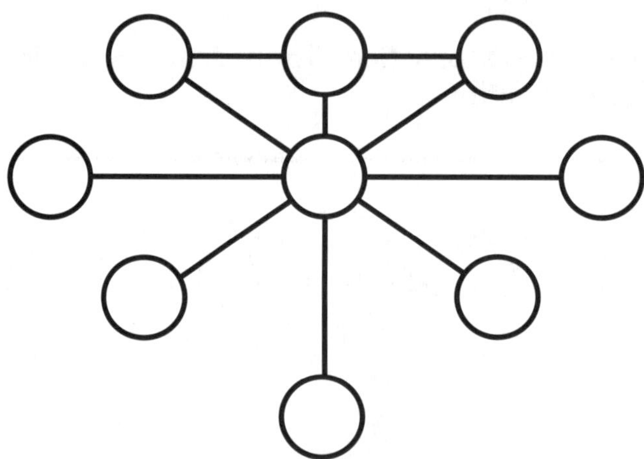

Arrange the numerals 1 through 9 in the boxes so that the sum of each side of the triangle equals 20.

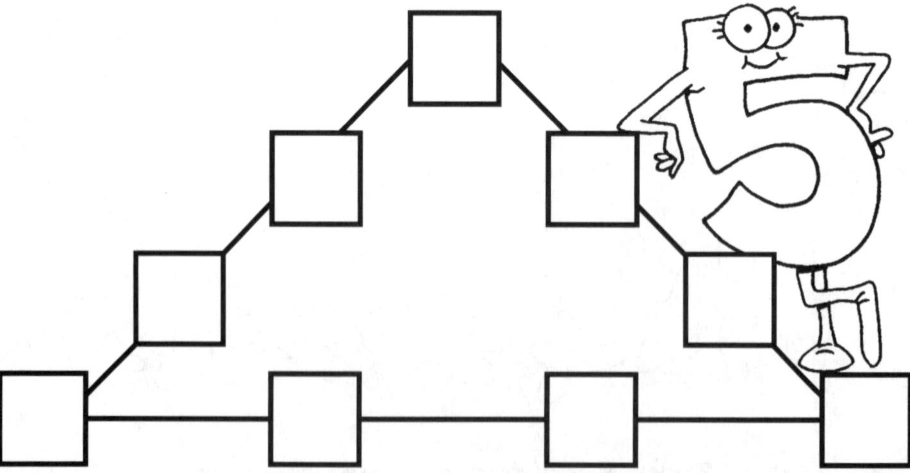

© Instructional Fair • TS Denison

Make It Thirty!

Fill in the missing math symbols to make each equation total 30. You may use +, −, x, or ÷.

1. 4 ( ) 5 ( ) 10 = 30
2. 5 ( ) 1 ( ) 6 = 30
3. 18 ( ) 8 ( ) 3 = 30
4. 15 ( ) 3 ( ) 6 = 30
5. 30 ( ) 5 ( ) 5 = 30

6. 60 ( ) 4 ( ) 2 = 30

7. 100 ( ) 10 ( ) 20 = 30

8. 100 ( ) 20 ( ) 6 = 30

9. 150 ( ) 5 ( ) 1 = 30

10. 40 ( ) 8 ( ) 6 = 30

Brain Booster: Use each symbol once to make the equation true.

10 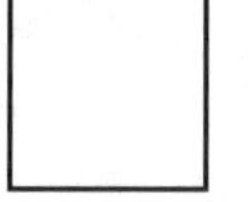 10 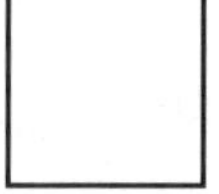 15  5 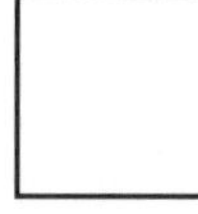 3 = 30

© Instructional Fair • TS Denison

Crossnumber Puzzle

Solve each equation to complete the crossnumber puzzle.

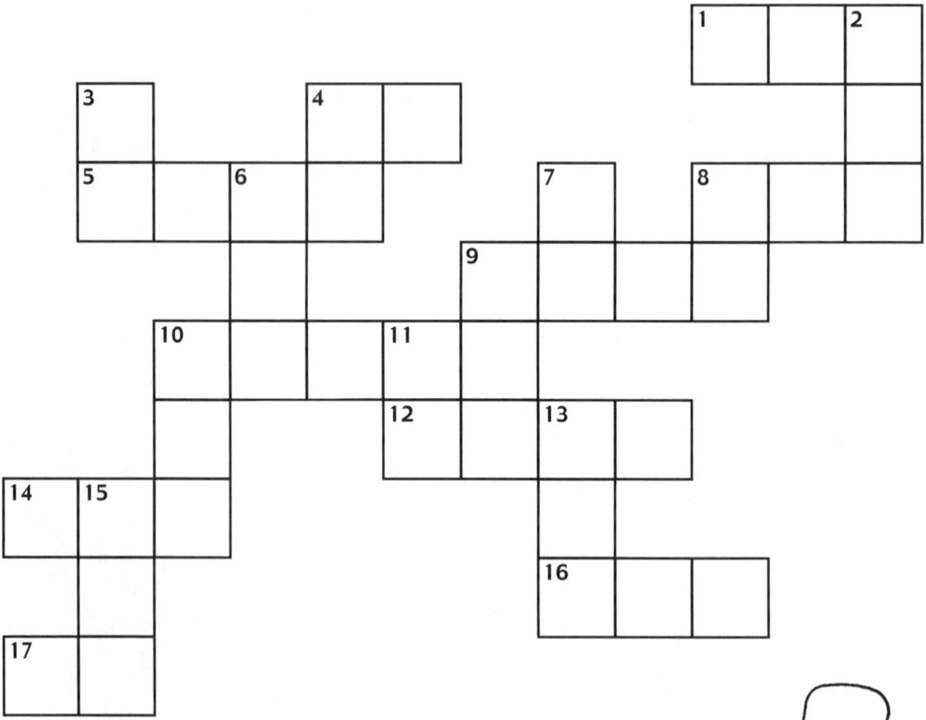

									1		2
	3			4							
	5		6				7		8		
						9					
		10			11						
					12		13				
14	15										
							16				
17											

Across:

1. 942 ÷ 2
4. 100 – 7
5. 4,000 + 36
8. 471 + 308
9. 231 x 40
10. 10,000 + 410
12. 265 x 5
14. 432 x 2
16. 135 x 4
17. 15 x 6

Down:

2. 13 x 13
3. 42 x 2
4. 45 + 51
6. 80 x 4
7. 13 + 19
8. 35 x 2
9. 301 x 3
10. 12 x 12
11. 121 ÷ 11
13. 15 x 15
15. 60 x 11

© Instructional Fair • TS Denison

Bull's-Eye Math

analysis

Each child threw three darts at the bull's-eye. Given the total score, can you figure out how many of each target each child hit? (Some clues are given.)

	5	10	15	25	TOTAL
Donna					75
Darnell					15
Hannah			1		25
Alex					65
James	1				30
Enrique					60
Karl			1		45
Amy					50
Tamika	1				25
Nina			1		35
Katja					55
Nick					40

Brain Booster: Make a list of all the possible totals for the dart scores. How many different ways could the children have scored?

© Instructional Fair • TS Denison

Climb the Mountain

Beginning with the bottom row, add each number pair. Write each total in the circle above the numbers. Work your way up the mountain until you reach the top. Your final sum should be 471. If it is not, go back and find where you made a mistake. Happy climbing!

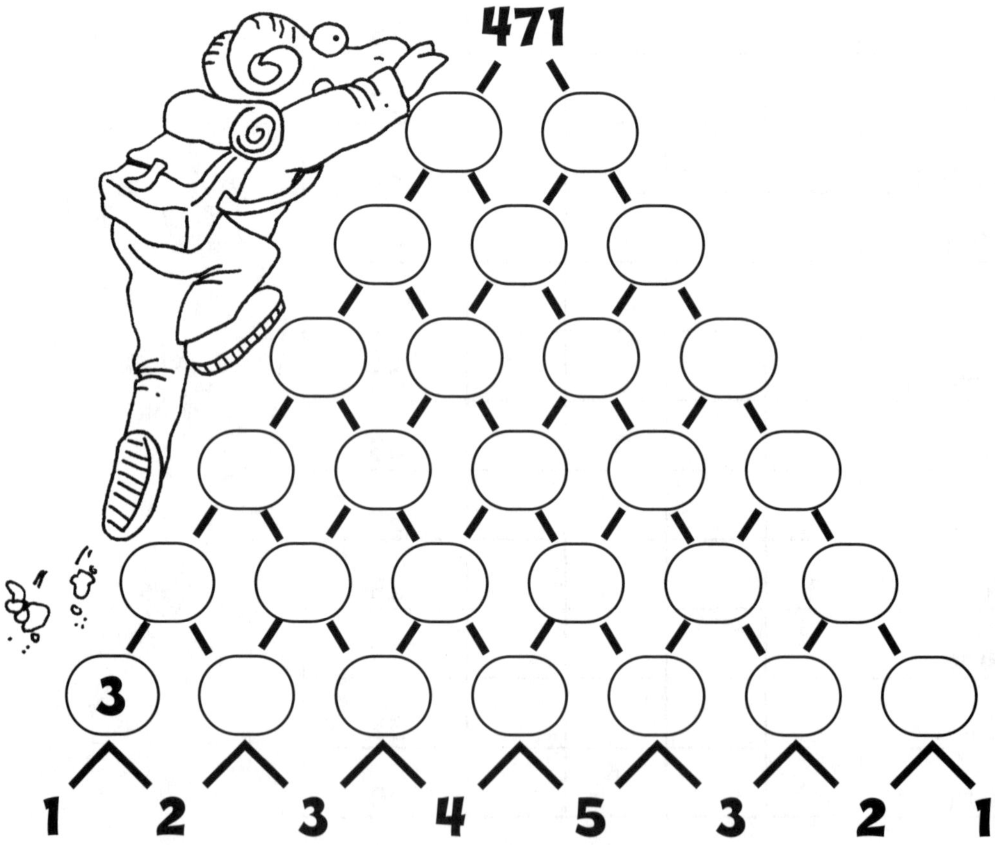

471

3

1 2 3 4 5 3 2 1

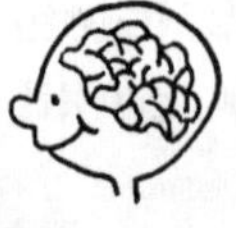

Brain Booster: Create another addition mountain using different numbers along the bottom.

© Instructional Fair • TS Denison

A Magic Trick

Do you like magic tricks? Here is a number trick you can memorize and show to your friends and family. Follow the directions carefully to discover how the trick works.

Example

1. Write a number that contains three different digits. **456**

2. Reverse the order of the digits. **654**

3. Subtract the smaller number from the larger number.

$$\begin{array}{r} 654 \\ -\ 456 \\ \hline 198 \end{array}$$

4. Add the digits of the answer. **1 + 9 + 8 = 18**

Repeat this trick three more times. Do you see a pattern? Once you understand how the trick works, use it to amaze your family and friends!

Just for Fun: Write the number 18 on a piece of paper. Have a friend hold up the paper while you perform the trick. When you get to the end, say, "Please read out loud the number I gave you before we began this magic trick." Everyone will be amazed. Don't repeat the trick or they will catch on.

© Instructional Fair • TS Denison

A Game for One

The object of this game is to land on the center space. Place a penny on any outside space. Then roll one die. Move horizontally or vertically the number indicated on the die. The center counts as a space if you must cross it. How many rolls of the die does it take you to reach the center? It may be harder than it sounds.

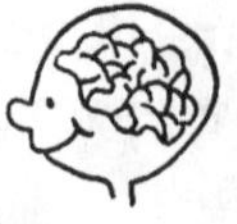

Brain Booster: Play this game with a friend, following the same rules. Race to the center.

© Instructional Fair • TS Denison

Origami Snake

synthesis

Follow the directions below to make an origami snake. Begin with a square sheet of paper that is not too thick. Fold along the dotted lines in the direction of the arrows.

1

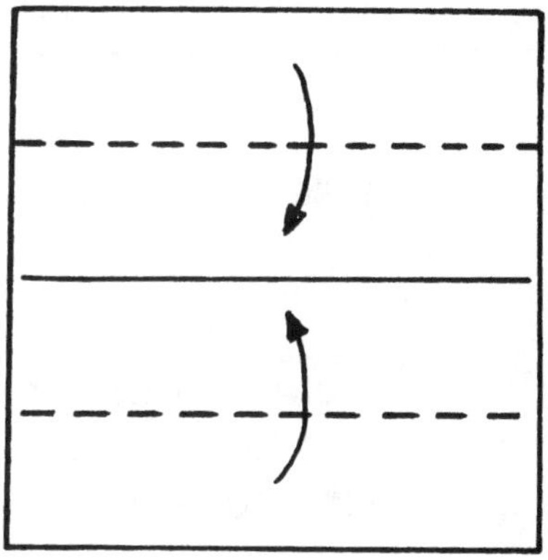

2

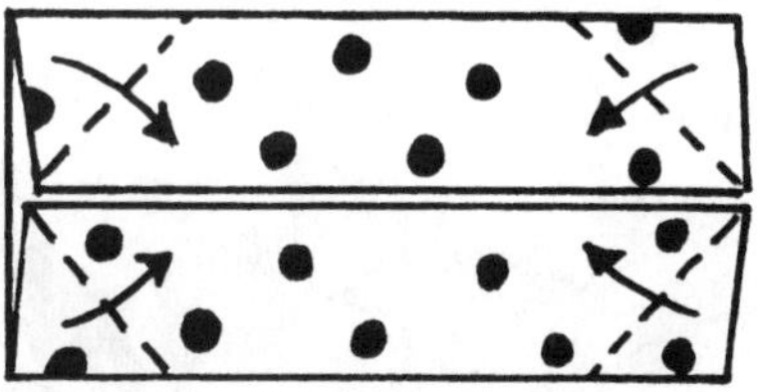

3

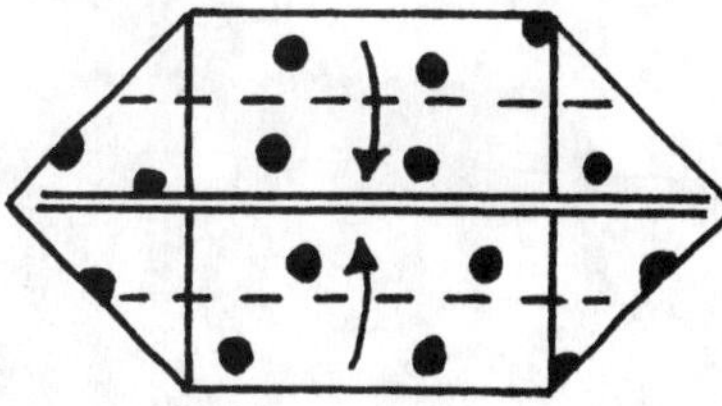

4

5

6

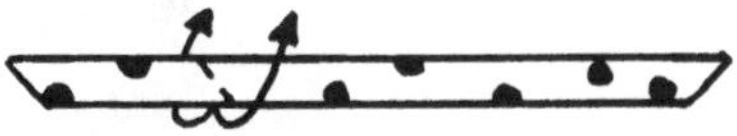

7

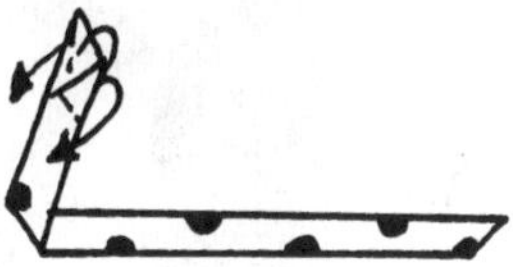

8

9

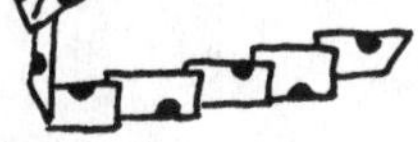

Just for Fun: Make several origami snakes in different colors and sizes. Add stripes or spots to your paper before you begin folding.

© Instructional Fair • TS Denison

Sunset Silhouettes

Choose a clear night to watch the sunset. Try to remember the vivid colors of the sky and the shapes of clouds along the horizon. Then turn that image into a painting. You will need: watercolor paints, a paint-brush, watercolor paper, water, black construction paper, scissors, and glue.

1. Paint a watercolor picture of the sunset you watched. Allow your painting to dry.

2. Once your painting is dry, add silhouettes to the scene. Cut images from black paper and glue onto your painting. Include things you see when looking at the horizon.

Answer Key

p. 5—Who Ordered Pizza?
Alice—chicken
Jason—burger
Marco—pizza

p. 6—Word Associations
1. gumball—not something you throw
2. sock—not a type of shoe
3. camera—not a time-keeper OR watch—does not begin with "C"
4. hat—not a body part OR foot—does not begin with "H"
5. cherry—not a citrus fruit
6. bed—does not have wheels OR jeep—does not begin with "B"
7. toupee—not made of glass
8. lawyer—not a medical doctor
9. book—not used to carry things OR purse—does not begin with "B"
10. refrigerator—does not heat things up

p. 7—Anagram Zoo

ant	tan
ape	pea
bat	tab
bear	bare
deer	reed
doe	ode
dog	god
eel	lee
foal	loaf
goat	toga
hare	hear
horse	shore
lamb	balm
owl	low
rat	tar
seal	sale
slug	lugs
snail	nails
snake	sneak
wasp	paws
wolf	flow

p. 8—Rebus Ending
"She was in a class by herself. It is not often that someone comes along who is a true friend and a good writer. Charlotte was both."

Brain Booster: Charlotte's Web

p. 9—Who Owns Which Pet?
Luis—parrot
Hannah—frog
Martin—dachshund
Kathy—cat

p. 10—Relating
Answers may vary.

1. baby	7. box
2. human	8. horse
3. bird	9. bull
4. horse	10. brush
5. refrigerator	11. winter
6. finger	12. butterfly

p. 13—Phonics Code

1. before	10. plate
2. afford	11. band
3. tooth	12. ease
4. wise	13. excel
5. bait	14. state
6. appease	15. form
7. fries	16. accuse
8. wonder	17. dates
9. seasoned	18. tepee

Brain Booster: Before you accuse Jay, question Mark.

p. 14—Compound Fun

1. butterfly	5. skateboard
2. honeycomb	6. skyscraper
3. horseshoe	7. toadstool
4. quarterback	8. turtleneck

p. 15—Car Search
Answers will vary.

p. 18—Paradise

```
T C T O M I D H J E N A X O K I S
O P A X R Y L C A S H E W S R T N
M T P I N E A P P L E S P A Y Q U
A N D C F B V N N K G Y A M N S S
T B K H E Y C I C T H E P G B T E
O E O R A N G E S L D R A E C O R
E A M J N D C O R N O R Y O R N I
S N P F J H T M U S P S A L S D C
V S O G E A B A N A N A S A I U E
C A V O C A D O E S I N G O P C Z
```

p. 20—More Pet Parade
1. Zigfried
2. toucans
3. Oscar
4. flat as dust
5. kangaroo
6. inched along, leaving an icky track
7. flew
8. emu
9. Harry and his high-stepping hippopotamus
10. Ralph

p. 21—Say It with a Simile

p. 22—A to Z Names
Answers will vary.

p. 23—Homonym Help
For two weeks I have been baking cakes with red icing. I cannot waste flour and sugar, so I ate every one of the cakes. Of course, my waist is getting bigger. I am getting as big as a horse. The plain fact is, I blew my diet.

p. 24—Onomatopoetry

d—hiss	e—pop	f—whine
c—howl	b—sizzle	a—whir

Answers will vary.
1. honk—goose, car horn
2. thump—bag dropped on floor, bass from a car radio
3. buzz—bumblebee, chainsaw
4. snap—fingers, stepping on a branch

p. 25—Line Design
Line designs will vary.

p. 26—How Old?
1. Javier is 6 years old.
   Luisa is 2 years old.
2. Father is 60 years old.
   Son is 20 years old.
3. Leo is 9 years old.
   James is 13 years old.

Brain Booster: Abby is also 6 years old. She was born just after her twin sister.

p. 27—Coordinate It

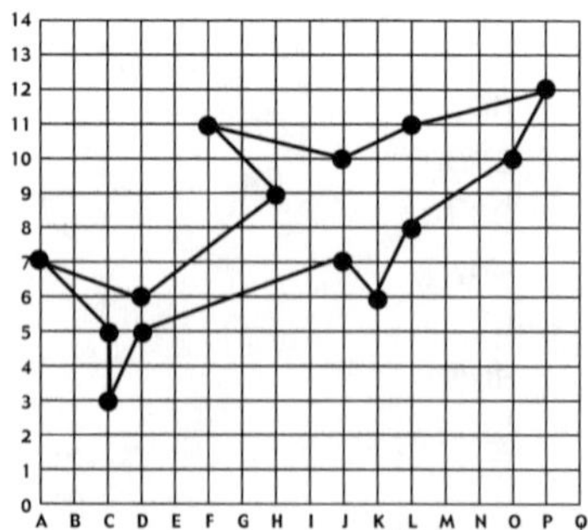

© Instructional Fair • TS Denison

p. 28—The Shape of Things

1. 3 toothpicks 3 marshmallows
2. 4 toothpicks 4 marshmallows
3. 5 toothpicks 5 marshmallows
4. 8 toothpicks 8 marshmallows
5. cube
6. pyramid

Brain Booster: 20 marshmallows
30 toothpicks

The shape is called a *dodecahedron*.

p. 29—Star Connection

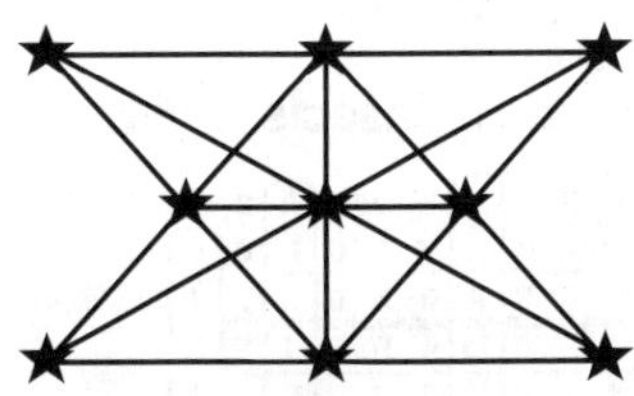

p. 30—It All Adds Up!

Arrangement of numbers may vary.

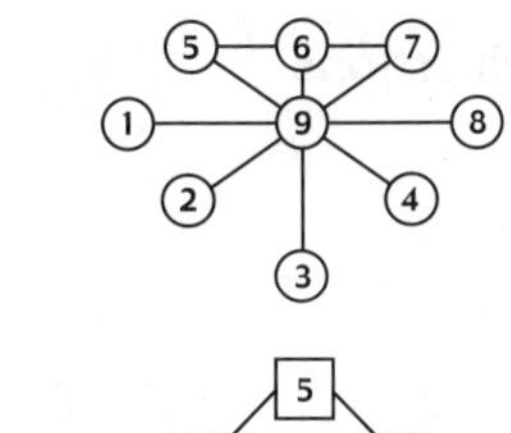

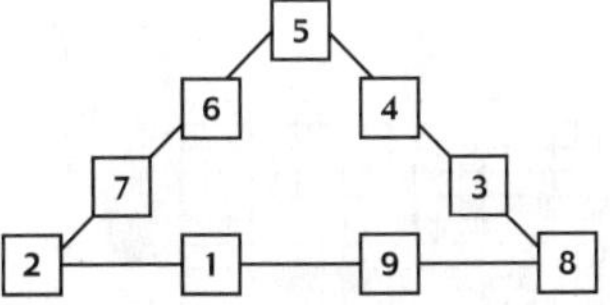

p. 31—Make It Thirty!

1. 4 × 5 + 10 = 30
2. 5 × 1 × 6 = 30
3. 18 − 8 × 3 = 30
4. 15 ÷ 3 × 6 = 30
5. 30 − 5 + 5 = 30
6. 60 ÷ 4 × 2 = 30
7. 100 ÷ 10 + 20 = 30
8. 100 ÷ 20 × 6 = 30
9. 150 ÷ 5 × 1 = 30
10. 40 ÷ 8 × 6 = 30

p. 31 (continued)

Brain Booster:

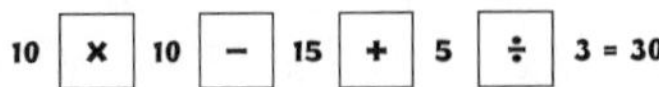

p. 32—Crossnumber Puzzle

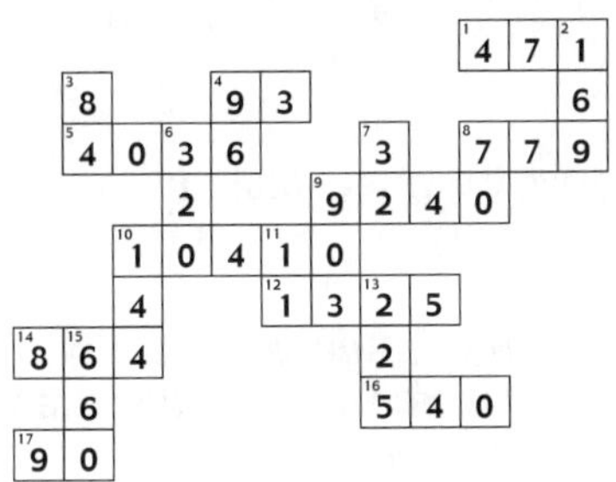

p. 33—Bull's-Eye Math

	5	10	15	25	TOTAL
Donna				3	75
Darnell	3				15
Hannah	2		1		25
Alex			1	2	65
James	1	1	1		30
Enrique		1		2	60
Karl	1		1	1	45
Amy		1	1	1	50
Tamika	1	2			25
Nina		2	1		35
Katja	1			2	55
Nick	1	1		1	40

p. 34—Climb the Mountain

471
233 238
109 124 114
48 61 63 51
20 28 33 30 21
8 12 16 17 13 8
3 5 7 9 8 5 3
1 2 3 4 5 3 2 1

p. 52—Name That Vegetable

1. carrot
2. asparagus
3. broccoli
4. spinach
5. corn
6. celery
7. onion
8. potato

p. 58—More Rumpelstiltskin

Answers will vary.

p. 59—Even More Rumpelstiltskin

Here are 100 words to get you started. This list is not complete.

elm	lime	pile	sink
ilk	limp	pill	sit
ill	link	pin	site
imp	lisp	pink	skill
impress	list	pistil	skin
in	litter	pit	skirt
ink	lurk	plum	slim
insert	melt	prim	slime
instill	mile	pun	slip
insult	mill	punt	slump
irk	milk	put	slurp
is	mink	putt	smile
isle	mitt	reins	spurt
it	must	rent	stem
kelp	mutt	rest	step
kill	mutter	rim	stilts
kilt	nest	rink	stink
kin	net	rip	stump
kink	nip	run	stun
kit	nut	runt	sun
kite	pelt	rust	tell
kitten	pen	rut	test
knelt	perk	sell	tin
knit	perm	silk	tire
krill	pest	sill	trim

p. 61—Just Ducky

ugly	homely
mean	vicious
kind	generous
beautiful	elegant

p. 63—More Sour Grapes

1. Snow White
2. Hansel and Gretel
3. Winnie the Pooh
4. Cinderella
5. The Little Red Hen
6. Little Jack Horner
7. Little Miss Muffet
8. The Three Bears

p. 68—Comparing Insects

W	C	R	I	C	K	E	T	F	I	G	A	D	E
A	H	T	O	M	L	W	E	V	A	U	P	O	C
S	L	N	C	O	C	K	R	O	A	C	H	Z	I
P	R	A	Y	I	N	G	M	A	N	T	I	S	C
R	A	K	G	R	I	B	I	D	V	J	D	K	A
H	Y	L	F	R	E	T	T	U	B	C	G	E	D
O	F	L	E	A	K	Y	E	O	H	S	M	I	A
A	N	T	D	X	O	B	E	E	T	L	E	Q	P

p. 70—Finding Directions

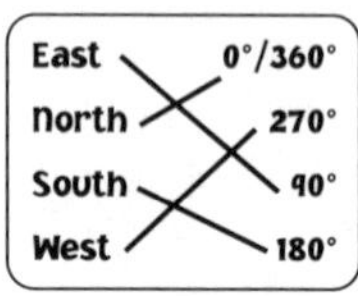

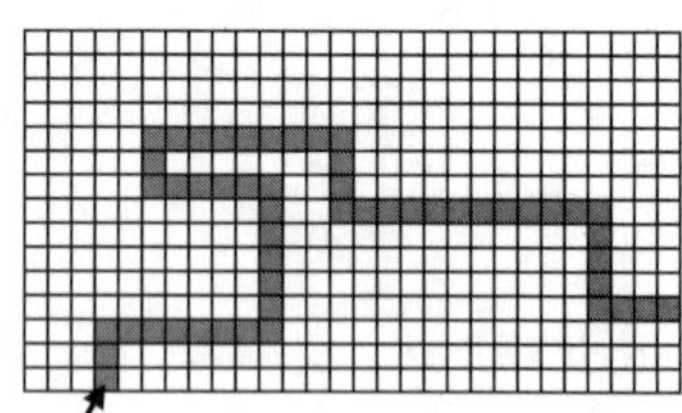

Galimoto

Galimoto is a type of push toy made by children in Malawi. You can make your own galimoto. You will need: heavy wire, pipe cleaners, cardboard, tape, and a long straight stick.

1. Look at pictures of cars, planes, trains, and other vehicles. Note the shapes that are most common.

2. Choose one type of vehicle and make a line drawing of it.

3. Use wire, pipe cleaners, and pieces of cardboard to create a 3-D version of your drawing. Bend and tape elements as needed to hold them together.

4. Since this is a push toy, be sure any wheels you make actually turn.

5. Attach a long stick to your toy. Use the stick to move the toy around.

Here are some vehicles to try:

- ambulance
- sailboat
- bulldozer
- helicopter
- fire truck
- dump truck
- cruise ship
- submarine
- flying saucer
- tugboat
- airplane
- taxicab
- train
- bus
- van

© Instructional Fair • TS Denison

synthesis

Clean Mud

Play with "clean mud" without getting your hands dirty! You will need: 3 rolls white toilet paper, 1 bar Ivory® soap* (grated), ¾ cup (178 ml) borax, a large plastic tub, a fine screen or cheesecloth, water, and poster paints.

1. Unroll the toilet paper into a large plastic tub. Add water until paper is just covered. Let sit overnight.

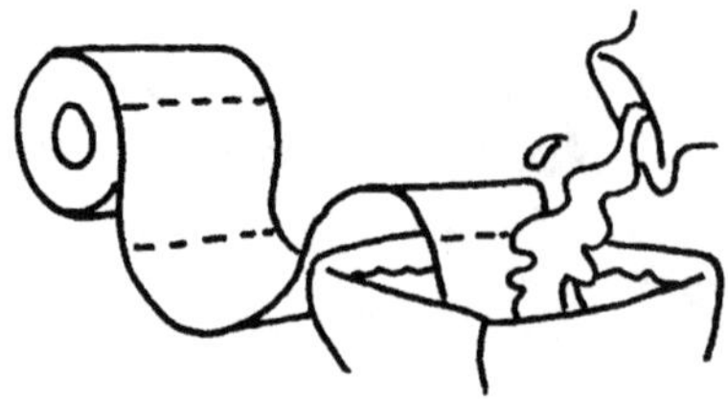

2. Add soap and borax. Stir. If the mud seems too wet, drain over a fine screen or cheesecloth, but don't squeeze.

3. Use the clean mud to make a landscape on a board. Cover the board completely, then add hills and mountains.

4. Let your landscape dry and harden. Once it is dry, paint the landscape with poster paints.

Just for Fun: Add small plastic people, animals, or other objects to your scene.

** Ivory is a registered trademark of Procter & Gamble.*

© Instructional Fair • TS Denison

A Two-Day Garden

Grow a crystal garden in just two days. You will need: a clear glass dish, food coloring, salt, laundry bluing (found in the laundry section of most supermarkets), and small bits of charcoal, brick, or sponge.

1. Put bits of charcoal, brick, or sponge in the bottom of a glass dish.
2. Sprinkle 2 tablespoons (25 ml) each of water, salt, and laundry bluing over the top.
3. Add a few drops of food coloring.
4. Set in a dry place.

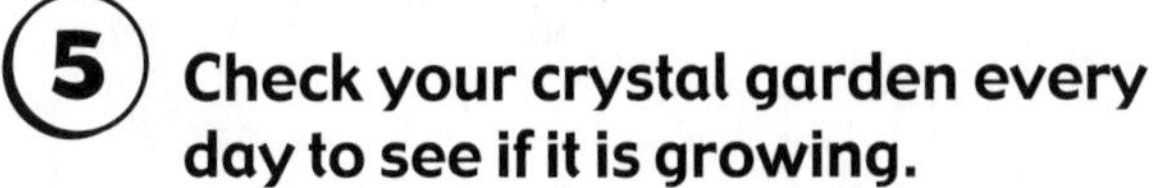

5. Check your crystal garden every day to see if it is growing.

Just for Fun: Draw butterflies, dragonflies, and ladybugs on heavy paper. Cut out and color both sides. Attach to paper clips and stand up in your crystal garden.

© Instructional Fair • TS Denison

Metal Wind Chime

Create your own wind chime. You will need: a branch or piece of driftwood, string, scissors, and various metal objects such as spoons, bells, and keys.

1. Gather a variety of metal objects found in your home. Tap things against each other to determine which objects make nice sounds.

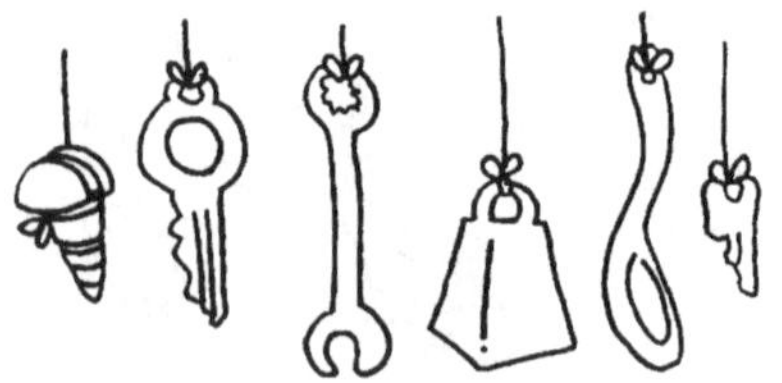

2. Attach each metal object to a piece of string at least 12" (30 cm) in length.

3. Tie each string to a branch. There should be some space between objects as they hang from the branch, and some objects may be hung at different lengths.

4. Cut a long piece of string. Attach to both ends of the branch. Use to hang from a hook outside or inside near a door or window. A slight wind or other movement will set your chime in motion.

© Instructional Fair • TS Denison

Design a City

Plan and create a model of an ideal city. Begin by sketching your ideas below. Then build a 3-D model. Use cardboard or balsa wood to make buildings and other structures. Create roads and sidewalks with masking tape or colored paper. Use your imagination!

My Ideal City

Just for Fun: Take photographs of your ideal city. Paste them in a notebook along with descriptions of your ideas and details about the city.

© Instructional Fair • TS Denison

Make Music!

Make the instruments on pages 44 and 45. Then grab some friends and form your own band.

Bass Fiddle

You will need: a coffee can, a hammer, a nail, a broomstick or a large dowel, string, and heavy tape.

1. Use a hammer and a nail to punch a hole in the bottom of the coffee can. Thread the string through the hole and tie a knot inside the can.
2. Tie the other end of the string to one end of the broomstick. Secure with string or heavy tape to keep it from sliding down.
3. To play, put one foot on the can to hold it in place. Rest the free end of the broomstick on the coffee can. Tilt the stick back until the string is tight and pluck the string.

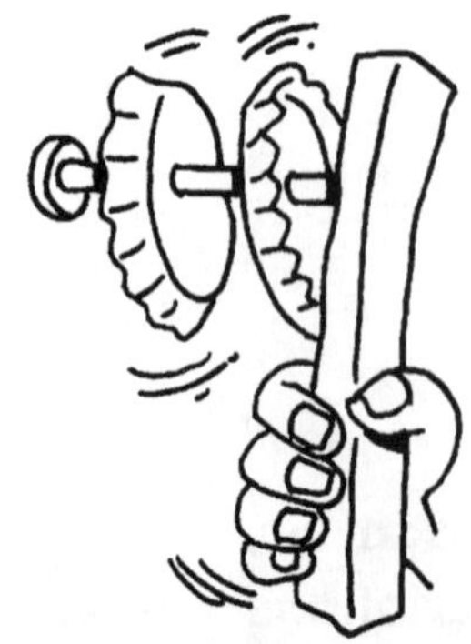

Bottle-Cap Rattle

You will need: six or eight metal bottle caps, a small piece of wood, nails, and a hammer.

1. Use a hammer and nail to punch a hole in the center of each bottle cap.
2. Nail two caps back-to-back (loosely) to a small piece of wood. Add other bottle caps the same way. Shake the rattle to the beat.

More Music Making!

Use these instruments with those on page 44 to create your own original music.

Panpipe

You will need: six plastic drinking straws, a strip of heavy paper about ¾" x 12" (2 cm x 30 cm), scissors, glue, and markers.

1. Decorate the strip of paper with markers.
2. Cut the six straws so that each is a different length. No straw should be less than 1" (3 cm) long. Arrange the straws from longest to shortest and lay them side by side.

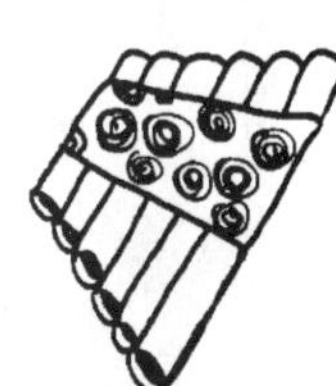

3. Align top edges of straws and glue to the back of the paper. Both ends of each straw should stick out.
4. Wrap the paper around the center of the straws, keeping them flat. Let dry. Play the panpipe by gently blowing air over the tops of the straws. Lips need not touch the straws.

Tambourine

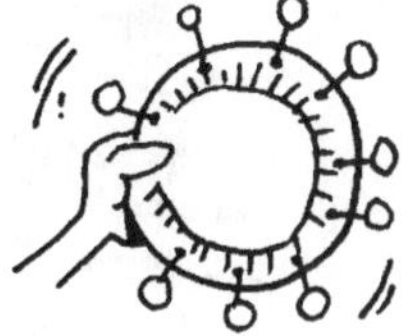

You will need: an aluminum pie pan, bottle caps or small bells, string, a hammer, and a nail.

1. Use a hammer and nail to punch holes along the outside of the pie pan.
2. Use a hammer and nail to punch a hole in the center of each bottle cap.
3. Tie each bottle cap or small bell to the pie pan with string.

Just for Fun: Create other instruments, such as maracas, drums, and cymbals, to help complete your band.

© Instructional Fair • TS Denison

synthesis

Who Are You?

Create a collage that shows what makes you unique. Use the space below to list your special qualities and things you like to do. Then draw pictures, write phrases or sentences, and glue cutouts from magazines onto a large sheet of poster board to create your collage.

Just for Fun: Create another poster about yourself using only words or phrases cut from old magazines.

© Instructional Fair • TS Denison

Make a Mad Meal

The next time you feel angry, go into the kitchen and make a mad meal. It might make you feel better. Use one of the following recipes, or make up your own.

Chunky Chopped Sandwiches

6 oz. (177 ml) can chunk white chicken, drained
1 small red apple
1 celery stalk
½ cup (118 ml) walnuts
3 tbsp. (45 ml) mayonnaise
1 tsp. (5 ml) cinnamon

Use a butter knife and lots of energy to cut the chicken, apple, and celery into small pieces. Mix together with remaining ingredients. Then stuff into a pita pocket or spread between two slices of bread.

Aggression Cookies

3 cups oatmeal
1 ½ cups (355 ml) brown sugar
1 ½ cups (355 ml) flour
1 tbsp. (15 ml) baking powder
1 ½ cups (355 ml) butter

Dump ingredients into a large mixing bowl. Mash, knead, and pound the mixture. The more you mix it, the better it will taste. Roll dough into small balls. Bake on cookie sheet at 350° F (177° C) for 10 to 12 minutes. Let cool before eating.

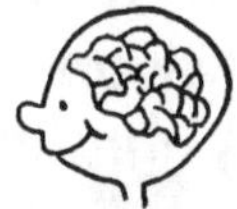

Brain Booster: Create your own recipes to relieve stress.

© Instructional Fair • TS Denison

analysis

Icky Biscuits

Why do biscuits double in size when they bake? Conduct this experiment to discover the answer. You will need: baking soda, vinegar, and flour.

1. What do you think will happen if you mix 1 tbsp. (15 ml) vinegar and 1 tbsp. (15 ml) baking soda in a bowl?

   Write your guess here: ____________________

   Now try it. What actually happened? ____________________

   ____

2. What do you think will happen if you add 1 tbsp. (15 ml) flour to the mixture?

   Write your guess here: ____________________

   Now try it. What actually happened? ____________________

   ____

3. What do you think will happen if you make a ball out of the dough and heat it in the microwave on HIGH for one minute?

   Write your guess here: ____________________

   Now try it. Analyze what happened. ____________________

   ____

Caution: Do not eat these biscuits. They taste awful!

Just for Fun: Using a recipe, assemble everything you need to make real biscuits for your family. Ask an adult to supervise as you make the treat for your dinner.

© Instructional Fair • TS Denison

Taste Bud Test

Your taste buds can distinguish four different flavors: sweet, salty, sour, and bitter. Design an experiment to determine where each type of taste bud is located. List the objective of your experiment, your hypothesis, the materials you will need, and the procedure you will follow. Then carry out your experiment.

Objective: ______________________________

Hypothesis: ______________________________

____

Materials: ______________________________

____

____

____

Procedure: ______________________________

____

____

____

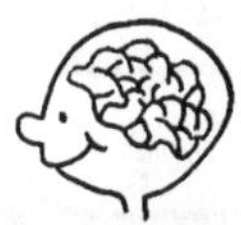

Brain Booster: Record your results. Draw a diagram to show your findings.

© Instructional Fair • TS Denison

evaluation

Backyard Cupcakes

Make cupcakes that look like they were scooped out of your backyard. You will need: a chocolate cake mix, additional ingredients needed for the recipe, cupcake pans, paper baking cups, a mixing bowl, a wooden spoon, and measuring cups.

1. Assemble the cake mix, necessary ingredients, and cooking utensils.

2. Follow directions on the box to make the batter. Pour into paper baking cups. Bake. Have an adult help you remove finished cupcakes from the oven. Let cool.

3. Decorate your cupcakes. Use your imagination! Here are just a few ideas:

- Use chocolate icing to make sticky mud.
- Use chocolate cookie crumbs to make clumps of dirt.
- Use coconut flakes and green food coloring to make grass.
- Use candy to make worms and other backyard critters.

On a scale of 1 to 5 (5 being the best), how much did you like baking these cupcakes?

1 2 3 4 5

© Instructional Fair • TS Denison

Making Flubber

Make your own flubber. You will need: warm water, glue, borax, food coloring, mixing bowls, and spoons.

1. Mix solution #1 in a mixing bowl.
Mix solution #2 in a separate glass bowl.

Solution #1

1 ½ cups (355 ml) warm water
2 cups (474 ml) white glue
food coloring

Solution #2

4 tsp. (20 ml) borax
1 ⅓ cups (316 ml) warm water
(Mix in a glass bowl.)

2. Slowly pour solution #1 into solution #2, but do not mix or stir. Lift out the flubber.

What happened when you poured solution #1 into the bowl with solution #2? ______________________________

____

How does the flubber feel? ______________________________

How does the flubber smell? ______________________________

Does the flubber bounce? ______________________________

comprehension

Name That Vegetable

Vegetables are foods that come from plants. They can be bulbs, flower buds, leaves, roots, seeds, stems, or tubers. Answer each riddle below by writing the correct vegetable name.

1. I am an orange root of a plant. I am good for eyesight.
   What am I? ___ ___ ___ ___ ___ ___

2. I am a green or white stem of a plant. I am shaped like a spear.
   What am I? ___ ___ ___ ___ ___ ___ ___ ___ ___

3. I am the green flower buds of a plant.
   What am I? ___ ___ ___ ___ ___ ___ ___ ___

4. I am a green leaf of a plant. I am packed with iron.
   What am I? ___ ___ ___ ___ ___ ___ ___

5. I am the seeds of a plant. I can also be made into a salty snack.
   What am I? ___ ___ ___ ___

6. I am the pale green stem of a plant.
   What am I? ___ ___ ___ ___ ___ ___

7. I am the bulb of a plant. I have a very strong odor.
   What am I? ___ ___ ___ ___ ___

8. I am the tuber of a plant used to make a popular side dish.
   What am I? ___ ___ ___ ___ ___ ___

Just for Fun: Make a salad with your favorite vegetables. Can you identify what part of a plant each vegetable is?

© Instructional Fair • TS Denison

Apple Butter

What exactly is apple butter? Take a guess. Then find out by making your own. You will need: a slow cooker, one dozen apples, sugar, cinnamon, a serrated knife, and a cutting board.

1. On a cutting board, slice the apples in half and then into quarters. Remove the seeds and stems.

2. Place apple quarters in slow cooker. Add several spoonfuls each of sugar and cinnamon. Stir and cover. Cook on HIGH for four hours, stirring occasionally. Remove lid and keep cooking until the mixture has the consistency of jam.

3. Let the apple butter cool. Refrigerate in a jar with a tight-fitting lid.

Just for Fun: Apple butter is actually apple sauce that has been cooked longer to remove more of the fruit's juice. Try using other fruits and a slow cooker to make fruit butters. Design and create jar labels for your creations.

© Instructional Fair • TS Denison

Face Paint

synthesis

Face painting is fun and easy. Create your own face paint right in the kitchen. You will need: a muffin pan, shortening, flour, and food coloring.

1. In one section of a muffin pan, mix together 1 tbsp. (15 ml) shortening, 1 tsp. (5 ml) flour, and one drop of food coloring.

2. Repeat to make several colors in other sections of the muffin pan.

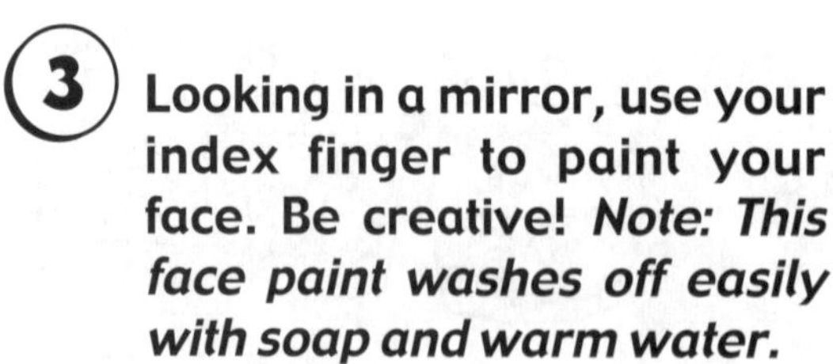

3. Looking in a mirror, use your index finger to paint your face. Be creative! *Note: This face paint washes off easily with soap and warm water.*

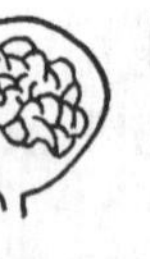

Brain Booster: Invite a friend over and paint each other's faces. Try to guess what the other person is painting before looking in a mirror.

© Instructional Fair • TS Denison

Peanut Butter Surprise

Have you ever had chocolate chip cookies with a peanut butter surprise in the middle? Make your own. You will need: a tube of chocolate chip cookie dough, a knife, peanut butter, and a cookie sheet.

1. Let the dough thaw while you assemble supplies.

2. Slice the dough into disks about ½" (13 mm) thick. Place nine disks on a cookie sheet. Pat flat.

3. Place a spoonful of peanut butter in the center of each slice of dough.

4. Use your fingers to wrap the dough around the peanut butter. Flatten slightly with the palm of your hand.

5. Bake at 350° F (177° C) for about ten minutes or until golden brown. Have an adult remove the hot baking sheet from the oven. Wait a few minutes before removing the cookies from the pan. Let cool on a wire rack.

On a scale of 1 to 5 (5 being the best), how good do you think these cookies taste?
1 2 3 4 5

© Instructional Fair • TS Denison

Bread Sculptures

Use bread dough to create sculptures. You will need: one package of frozen bread dough, flour, shortening, paper towels, and a baking sheet.

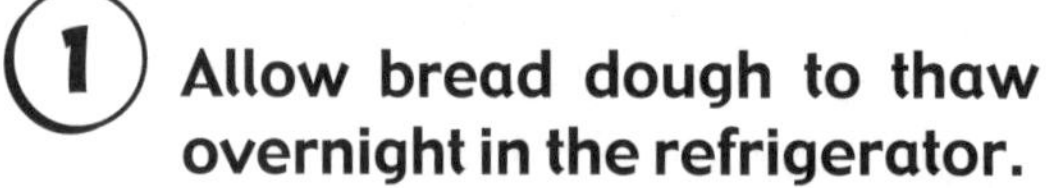

1. Allow bread dough to thaw overnight in the refrigerator.

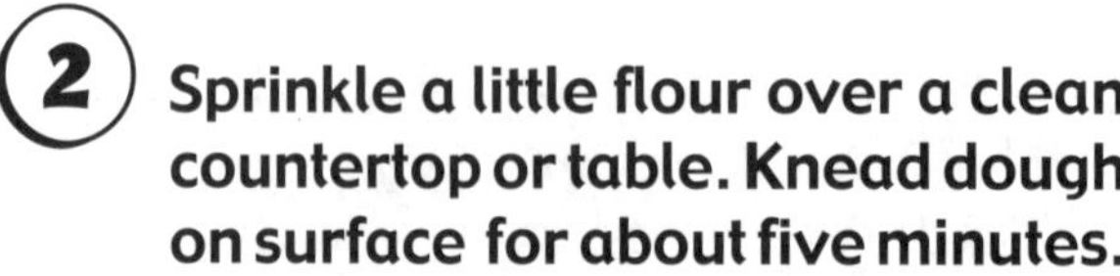

2. Sprinkle a little flour over a clean countertop or table. Knead dough on surface for about five minutes.
3. Divide the dough into four to six sections. Use the sections to create animals, people, letters, or other shapes. Lay flat on a greased baking sheet.

4. Cover the sculptures with paper towels and let rise thirty minutes.
5. Bake at 350° F (177° C) for about twenty minutes or until golden brown. Ask an adult to remove the sculptures from the oven. Let cool slightly before eating.

On a scale of 1 to 5 (5 being the best), how good do your bread sculptures taste?
1 2 3 4 5

Just for Fun: If you don't want to eat the sculptures, shellac them. They will keep for a long time.

© Instructional Fair • TS Denison

Rumpelstiltskin

Read the story of "Rumpelstiltskin."

Once there lived a poor miller who had a beautiful daughter. The miller was so proud of his child that he often exaggerated her talents. One day he told the king that his daughter could spin gold out of straw. Naturally, the king wanted to meet her.

The king sent for the miller's daughter and locked her in a chamber with a heap of straw and a spinning wheel. He told her to spin the straw to gold before morning. Of course, she did not know how and began to cry. Just then, a hobgoblin appeared. He agreed to spin the straw into gold in exchange for her necklace.

The king greedily accepted the heap of spun gold the next morning but quickly decided he wanted more. That night he left the miller's daughter with an even bigger pile of straw. Again, the same hobgoblin appeared, agreeing to spin the straw into gold in exchange for the girl's ring.

Once again, the king took the gold and demanded even more. This time when the hobgoblin appeared, the girl had nothing more to trade. Finally she agreed to give the hobgoblin her first child if only he would spin the last pile of straw into gold. When the king saw the gold the next morning, he married the girl and made her his queen.

One year later, the king and queen had their first child. When the hobgoblin came to collect the child, the queen begged for mercy. Being a prankster who enjoyed games, he made a deal with her. If she could guess his name, she could keep her child.

For three days the queen tried to guess the hobgoblin's name without success. Desperate, she sent a trusted servant in search of the hobgoblin to discover his name. Just before dawn, the servant found him deep in the forest, singing a song about his name, Rumpelstiltskin. When the hobgoblin appeared the next day to take the child, the queen called him by his name. He was so mad that he stomped his foot and ran off, never to be seen again.

© Instructional Fair • TS Denison

evaluation

More Rumpelstiltskin

Fairy tales are told to teach lessons. On a scale of 1 to 5 (1 being "poor" and 5 being "excellent"), rate this story's strength in teaching the following lessons.

____ 1. He who laughs last, laughs best.

____ 2. Never tell lies to people in power.

____ 3. Never make deals with strangers.

____ 4. Women can do anything.

____ 5. If you try hard enough, you can do anything.

____ 6. The best way to get a husband is to promise him gold

____ 7. Fathers who are proud of their children will often exaggerate their good qualities.

____ 8. Telling lies can get you into serious trouble.

____ 9. Like father, like daughter.

____ 10. Never trust someone who can turn straw into gold.

HA
HA
HA

Brain Booster: In your own words, write the most important lesson taught by "Rumpelstiltskin."

____

____

© Instructional Fair • TS Denison

Even More Rumpelstiltskin

Can you find 50 words in the name "Rumpelstiltskin"?
List them below.

1. ______
2. ______
3. ______
4. ______
5. ______
6. ______
7. ______
8. ______
9. ______
10. ______
11. ______
12. ______
13. ______
14. ______
15. ______
16. ______
17. ______
18. ______
19. ______
20. ______
21. ______
22. ______
23. ______
24. ______
25. ______
26. ______
27. ______
28. ______
29. ______
30. ______
31. ______
32. ______
33. ______
34. ______
35. ______
36. ______
37. ______
38. ______
39. ______
40. ______
41. ______
42. ______
43. ______
44. ______
45. ______
46. ______
47. ______
48. ______
49. ______
50. ______

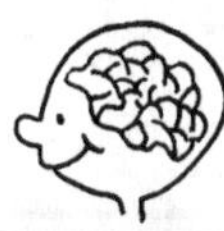

Brain Booster: Can you list 100 words? 250?
What is the longest word you can find?

The Ugly Duckling

Read the story of "The Ugly Duckling."

One late spring day, Mother Duck's eggs began to hatch. When the last egg broke, she gasped, "Oh my!" and watched as an ugly little duckling broke free of its shell. Her six fluffy babies and one ugly duckling grew through the long, lazy summer that followed.

The other barnyard animals teased the ugly duckling, though Mother Duck did her best to protect him from their cruel words. "Oh my," she sighed after a particularly mean attack. She stroked the duckling's neck and quacked his favorite song. When she finished, Mother Duck saw tears in the duckling's eyes. "Oh my," she sighed again, worried that he would soon leave her.

That night, the ugly duckling slipped away. He walked past the barn, past the pond, across the meadow, and into the forest. He walked all night until he reached the big lake on the far side of the forest. Exhausted, he lay down and cried himself to sleep.

Weeks passed, and the ugly duckling was miserable. He was always alone. Then one afternoon a flock of swans landed on the lake. Their songs stirred something deep within him—it was the most wonderful feeling he had ever known. Alas, the swans had gone by the next morning. The winter that followed was snowy and bitter cold.

One bright spring day, the sun began to shine and melt the snow. The swans returned, once again filling the sky. A beautiful swan swam up to the duckling and spoke kindly to him. At that moment, he caught sight of his own reflection in the water. To his surprise, he saw a handsome swan—not an ugly duckling. Filled with joy, he trumpeted the most beautiful song ever heard on the lake. His song soared through the forest, across the meadow, past the pond, and into the barnyard. The animals all stopped to listen to the beautiful music, but only one recognized the song. "Oh my," whispered Mother Duck, for at last she knew what had become of her ugly little duckling.

© Instructional Fair • TS Denison

Just Ducky

Complete the following activities related to the story.

Circle the synonym for each vocabulary word from the story.

ugly	humbly	hasty	homely	hosiery
mean	vicious	vigorous	various	valiant
kind	generate	generous	genius	general
beautiful	eloquent	elevate	element	elegant

Write one sentence using all four words you circled.

____

____

____

Create a comic strip based on the main character in "The Ugly Duckling." Tell a story in just eight frames. Plan the plot of your story here, then draw it out on a large sheet of poster board. Color with markers or paints. Give your comic strip a clever title.

Title: ____

© Instructional Fair • TS Denison

Sour Grapes

Read Aesop's fable, "The Fox and the Grapes."

Once there was a very hungry fox. The fox had not eaten in several days when he came upon a vineyard. All the grapes in the vineyard had been picked except for one large, juicy bunch hanging high on a trellis. The fox leaped for joy as he spotted the grapes.

The grapes, however, were out of the fox's reach. He tried for hours but could not jump high enough to grab them. Discouraged, he finally left the vineyard. "I am not very hungry anyway," he consoled himself. "Besides, I'm sure those grapes are sour."

Reenact the story with a friend, using the script below.

Narrator: As our story opens, a hungry fox is searching for his supper.

Fox: Woe is me. I am so hungry. I haven't eaten since last Sunday I am so famished, I can hardly walk.

Narrator: Poor fox, he looks desperate. Hopefully he will find somethin to eat soon.

Fox: Alas! A vineyard! I hope it is full of plump, sweet grapes.

Narrator: The fox hurries along the road and rushes into the vineyar only to find that the crop has already been plucked from th branches.

Fox: What! Not a grape in sight. Woe is me. I am too late.

Narrator: Poor fox, whatever will he do?

Fox: But wait. There, high above my head, what do I spy? Are thos grapes that I see, plump, purple, and dripping with juic sweeter than honey? Soon my stomach will be full!

Narrator: The fox was right. There was one bunch of grapes remaining.

Fox: *(Jumping and reaching, jumping and reaching.)* Drat! I canno reach the grapes.

Narrator: The fox was there for most of the afternoon, jumping an reaching, but to no avail. Finally, as the sun went down, the fo was too exhausted to go on. Saddened, he left the vineyard.

Fox: Oh, well. I am not that hungry, and besides, I'm sure those grapes are sour anyway.

© Instructional Fair • TS Denison

More Sour Grapes

The expression "sour grapes" often makes people think of the fable "The Fox and the Grapes." Match the foods below with the correct stories. Use the titles in the Name Bank to help you.

Name Bank:

Little Miss Muffet	Winnie the Pooh
Hansel and Gretel	The Three Bears
Little Jack Horner	Snow White
The Little Red Hen	Cinderella

1. Poison apple ____________________
2. Gingerbread house ____________________
3. Honey pot ____________________
4. Giant pumpkin ____________________
5. Wheat bread ____________________
6. Christmas pie ____________________
7. Curds and whey ____________________
8. Porridge ____________________

Brain Booster: List three more foods and the stories they are associated with.

© Instructional Fair • TS Denison

The Boy Who Cried Wolf

Read Aesop's fable, "The Boy Who Cried Wolf."

One day a little boy was watching his father's sheep. He soon became bored and cried, "Wolf! Wolf!" to add some excitement. Hearing his cries, the villagers came running with clubs and pitchforks. But they found no wolf and so returned home.

Several days later the boy was watching the sheep again. Bored once more, he cried, "Wolf! Wolf!" and everyone came running to the field. Once again, they found no wolf.

One day a wolf really did attack the flock. The boy cried for help, but the villagers did not come. They thought he was playing a prank. Without their help, the boy could not protect the sheep. The wolf ate every single sheep in the flock.

Write a short newspaper article describing the final event of the story. Try to be objective and report only the facts. Include quotes from the boy and some of the villagers.

Wolf Attacks and Kills Whole Flock of Sheep

© Instructional Fair • TS Denison

A Wolf in Sheep's Clothing

Animals are often associated with certain personality types. What personalities do you think the animals below would have? Cast them as characters in a story. Map out your story using the outline below. Make a puppet for each character and use to act out your story.

haracters:

Name: ______________________
Description: ______________________
Name: ______________________
Description: ______________________
Name: ______________________
Description: ______________________
Name: ______________________
Description: ______________________

etting: ______________________

roblem: ______________________

vents: ______________________

____

____

olution: ______________________

____

____

© Instructional Fair • TS Denison

synthesis

Listen!

Sound is carried by vibrations. Your outer ear (the part that you can see) catches sounds and makes them louder. Conduct this experiment to learn how the size and position of the outer ear can affect hearing.

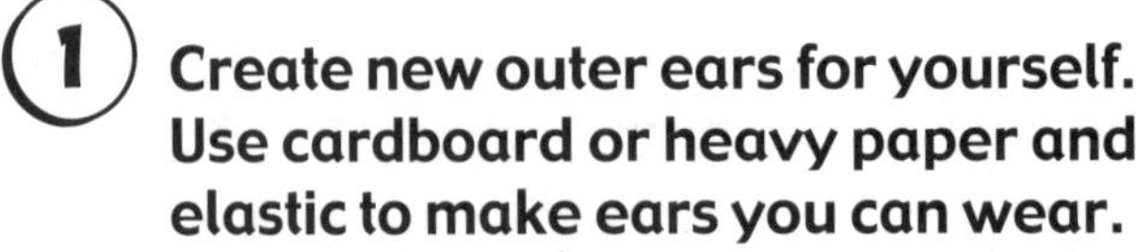

1. Create new outer ears for yourself. Use cardboard or heavy paper and elastic to make ears you can wear.

2. Locate different sources of noise in your home. Listen to each sound carefully for several seconds. Then listen to the same sound while cupping your ears towards the source. Finally, listen to the same sound while wearing your new-and-improved ears. How is the sound different each time?

3. Sit outside wearing your paper ears and list the sounds that you hear. Are there some sounds you can hear with your paper ears that you cannot hear with just your own ears?

4. Construct several different types of ears. Compare how well you hear with each kind. Draw the ears that help you hear the best. Can you think of an animal whose ears are similar in shape?

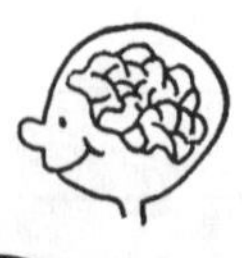

Brain Booster: The next time you are in the tub, lie down so your ears are underwater. Listen carefully. Do things sound different underwater? Talk or sing and see how your voice sounds different.

© Instructional Fair • TS Denison

A Terrarium

A terrarium is a small living ecosystem that contains everything a plant needs to survive: air, water, light, and food. The water comes from moisture in the soil and is recycled inside the container via the water cycle. Leaves that fall decompose in the soil, providing food for the roots of the plant.

Make your own terrarium. You will need: a large glass jar with lid, small pebbles, charcoal bits, potting soil, and small plants from your yard such as ferns or ivy.

1. Layer the materials as shown in a large glass jar.

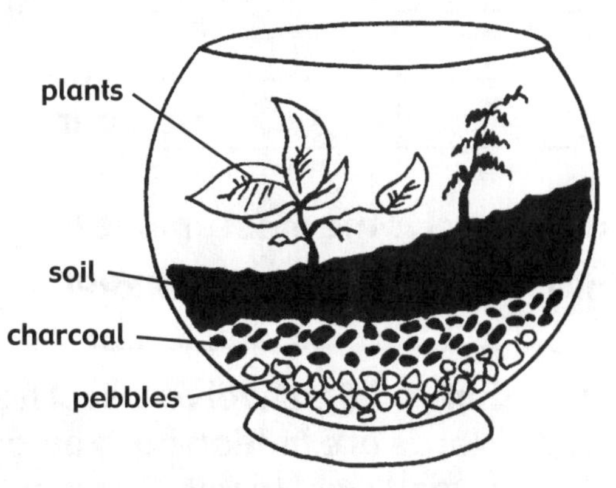

2. Add water to the soil until moist but not soggy.
3. Place the terrarium in a spot where it will receive indirect sunlight. Cover.
4. If moisture collects inside the terrarium, open the lid slightly.
5. Collect a small lizard or toad and add to your terrarium. Research how to care for your new pet. Release the animal after a few days.

Just for Fun: Add an earthworm to your terrarium to help break down dead matter in the soil.

© Instructional Fair • TS Denison

Comparing Insects

Collect six different insects. Put each in a separate jar with small holes punched in the lid. Study each insect to complete the chart below. Release the insects after you have finished your observation.

	kind	color	size	shape	# of legs	# of wings
1.						
2.						
3.						
4.						
5.						
6.						

Which insect is the most unique? ____________________

Which two are the most similar? ____________ and ____________

Can you find twelve insect names hidden in the puzzle? Words are hidden horizontally or vertically, and some read right to left. Circle each insect name you find.

W	C	R	I	C	K	E	T	F	I	G	A	D	E
A	H	T	O	M	L	W	E	V	A	U	P	O	C
S	L	N	C	O	C	K	R	O	A	C	H	Z	I
P	R	A	Y	I	N	G	M	A	N	T	I	S	C
R	A	K	G	R	I	B	I	D	V	J	D	K	A
H	Y	L	F	R	E	T	T	U	B	C	G	E	D
O	F	L	E	A	K	Y	E	O	H	S	M	I	A
A	N	T	D	X	O	B	E	E	T	L	E	Q	P

© Instructional Fair • TS Denison

Lightning Calculator

Have you ever watched a thunderstorm in the distance and wondered how far away it was? You can calculate the distance of a storm if you watch and listen carefully. You will need: a paper plate, markers, a piece of lightweight cardboard, scissors, a brad fastener, and a stopwatch or watch with a second hand.

1 Use a black marker to print the numbers 1–12 on the paper plate as shown. The black numbers represent miles. Multiply each number by five and write along the outer edge of the plate in red. The red numbers represent sec-

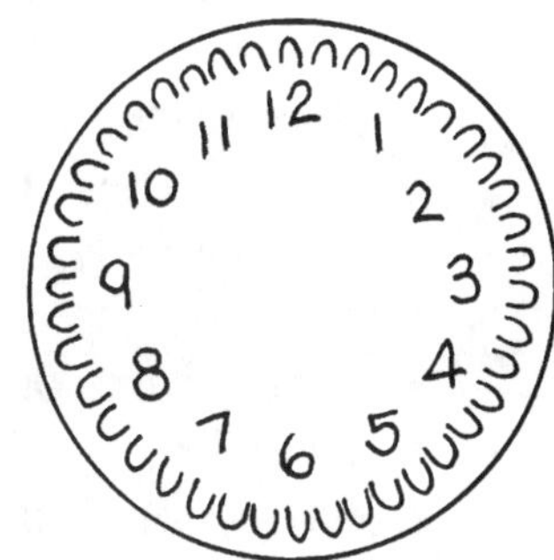

2 Cut three arrows from the cardboard. Label them 1, 2, and 3. Attach to the plate with a brad fastener.

3 From a safe place inside, use a stopwatch to count the number of seconds between a lightning flash and the sound of thunder.

4 Set the first arrow to the correct number of seconds (red). The black number will tell you how far away the storm is. (Multiply this number by 1.6 to find the distance in kilometers.)

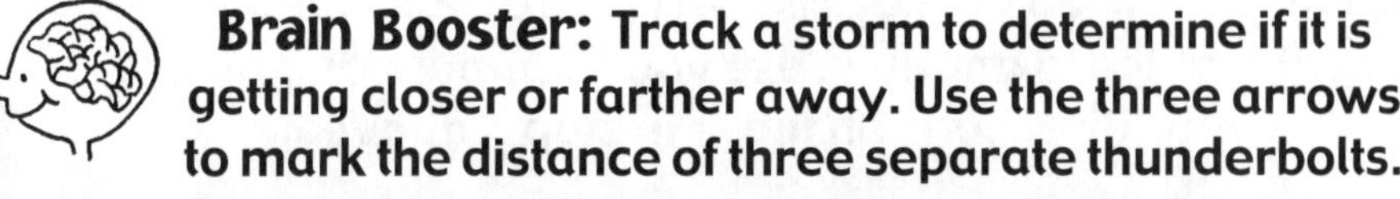

Brain Booster: Track a storm to determine if it is getting closer or farther away. Use the three arrows to mark the distance of three separate thunderbolts.

© Instructional Fair • TS Denison

Finding Directions

A compass is easy to use. It has a small, magnetized needle that turns freely and always points north. Once you find north, you can find other directions as well.

1. Hold a compass flat in your hand. Turn until the red end of the needle lines up with "N," and you will be facing north. What is directly east? What is directly west? What is directly south?

East	0°/360°
North	270°
South	90°
West	180°

2. The numbers on the compass represent the 360 degrees of a circle. The sign for a degree is °. In the box above, draw a line between each direction and the correct degree mark.

3. Follow the directions to draw a path. Begin at the arrow and color your path as you go. The path has been started for you.

N

□ = 5 paces

1. Go north 15 paces.
2. Go east 35 paces.
3. Go north 30 paces.
4. Go west 25 paces.
5. Go north 10 paces.
6. Go east 40 paces.
7. Go south 15 paces.
8. Go east 55 paces.
9. Go south 20 paces.
10. Go east 15 paces.

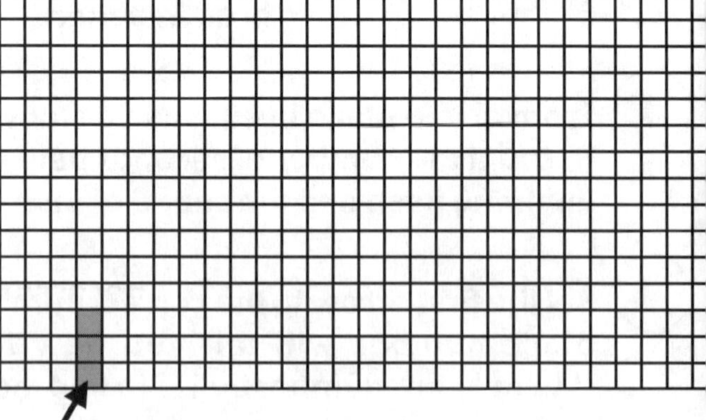

Just for Fun: Go outside and write directions for getting from one place to another. Use your compass and model your directions on those in step 3 above.

© Instructional Fair • TS Denison

Plan an Adventure

Synthesis

The outdoors can offer a range of adventures, from simply looking at leaves to hiking or camping. What is your favorite thing to do outside? Circle or write your answers to the questions below. Then plan your own adventure. Follow your completed plan and have fun!

1. What is your favorite time of the day to go outside?

   a. dawn b. morning c. noon d. dusk e. night

2. What are your favorite sights in your backyard?

   a. plants
   b. rocks
   c. animals
   d. sky
   e. soil

   List specifics:
   ____
   ____
   ____
   ____

3. What is your favorite way to experience the outdoors?

   a. look
   b. listen
   c. touch
   d. smell
   e. taste

   List specifics:
   ____
   ____
   ____
   ____

4. What is your favorite way to record outdoor adventures?

   a. write in a journal
   b. collect mementos
   c. talk about them
   d. think about them

5. Using everything you have circled or listed above, plan a backyard outing for yourself. List what you will do and when. Use another sheet of paper if necessary.

____
____
____
____
____

© Instructional Fair • TS Denison

analysis

Earthworm Observatory

Earthworms move by using muscles and tiny bristles called *setae*. Since they live in the ground and avoid daylight, they can be hard to observe, but it is easy to make your own earthworm observatory. You will need: earthworms, a tall plastic jar, soil, water, black paper, rubber bands, and food for the worms, including bits of grass, leaves, and lettuce.

1. Fill a tall plastic jar with soil. Add water to dampen the soil. If the soil is too wet, the worms may drown.

2. Collect several earthworms. They are easiest to find on a rainy day or at night. Place the worms in the jar.

3. Sprinkle bits of lettuce, grass, leaves, and coffee grounds on top of the soil.

4. Wrap the jar with black paper. Secure with two rubber bands.

5. Remove the paper the next day. What do you see? Record your observations in a notebook. Did the worms eat any food? Continue to observe the worms for several days. Keep the jar covered between observation times.

6. When you are done observing them, release the worms near the spot where you found them. How long does it take them to burrow back into the ground?

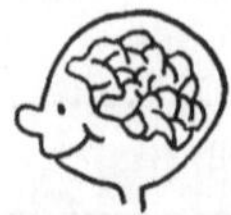

Brain Booster: Find out what your worms' favorite foods are.

© Instructional Fair • TS Denison

It's for the Birds

Bird feeders are easy to make. Try these variations, or design your own. You will need: a two-liter plastic bottle, a twig, birdseed, a pinecone, peanut butter, suet, and rope.

Feeder #1

1. Punch holes on opposite sides of a two-liter bottle. Stick a twig through both holes, leaving the ends to stick out as perches.
2. Poke other holes around the perches for birds to pull out seeds.
3. Fill bottle with birdseed and hang from a tree branch.

Feeder #2

1. Coat a pinecone with peanut butter, then suet.
2. Roll in birdseed.
3. Hang from a tree branch.

Try to identify the birds that visit your feeders. Check off each type of bird that you see. Circle the one you see the most. Draw or list the names of any other birds you see in a notebook.

____	blue jay	____	robin
____	chickadee	____	woodpecker
____	cardinal	____	sparrow
____	finch	____	yellow-bellied sapsucker

Observe how the birds interact.
Do some birds seem to chase others away?

© Instructional Fair • TS Denison

Be a Sky Watcher

There are many wonderful and mysterious things to observe in the sky. Go outside each day this month and look for the conditions described onpages 74 and 75.

Double Rainbow

A double rainbow is made up of a primary rainbow and a secondary rainbow. The secondary rainbow is a reflection of the primary rainbow. It is fainter in color and its colors are reversed.

Crepuscular Rays

Crepuscular rays are shafts of light that extend outward from the sun. They are most often seen at sunrise or sunset. (**Caution:** Shade your eyes when looking toward the sun. *Never* look directly at it.)

Short-Lived Clouds

During some fair-weather afternoons, small cumulus clouds form across the sky. These clouds have a relatively short lifespan. If you watch them closely, you will see that they disappear quickly—just minutes after forming.

Silver Lining

Thick, irregular, and scattered clouds sometimes have edges that shine brightly. This is called a cloud's "silver lining." Under certain conditions, near sunrise or sunset, this can become a golden lining.

© Instructional Fair • TS Denison

Be a Sky Watcher

knowledge

Halos

Halos are bright, often colorful rings, arcs, and spots around the sun. Halos generally appear red, orange, or yellow. (**Caution:** Shade your eyes when looking toward the sun. *Never* look directly at it.)

Sun Dogs

Sun dogs are bright, often colorful spots in cirrus clouds, ice fogs, or even blowing snow. They can form on both sides of the sun. They appear at the same altitude as the sun and are reddish on the side facing it. Look for bluish tails stretching horizontally away from the sun. Sun dogs are usually much brighter than halos.

Mirage

A mirage is an optical illusion, in which something appears that does not really exist. The image of the sun just rising or setting on the horizon is a mirage. The sun is actually below the line of direct sight to the horizon. Another common mirage is a pool of water on hot pavement.

Twinkling Star

Stars appear to twinkle when their light rays are bent (refracted) and dispersed while passing through air of varying density. It is most common on clear and windy nights. Stars near the horizon twinkle more than those directly overhead, because their light must pass through more atmosphere.

© Instructional Fair • TS Denison

synthesis

Blimp Scale

Build a blimp scale that you can use to compare the weights of small objects. You will need: a 1 pt. (474 ml) milk carton, scissors, a non-flexible drinking straw, three helium-filled balloons, thread, and tape.

1. Wash the milk carton with soapy water. Let dry. Cut in half lengthwise.
2. Tie two 18" (45 cm) pieces of thread to the straw.
3. Tape or tie the four ends of thread securely to the corners of the carton.

4. Tape or tie a long piece of thread or string to the carton.
5. Tape or tie the balloons to the straw. If your blimp floats to the ceiling, pull it down with the long string.
6. Try placing different objects in the milk carton to see what makes the blimp go up and what makes it go down.

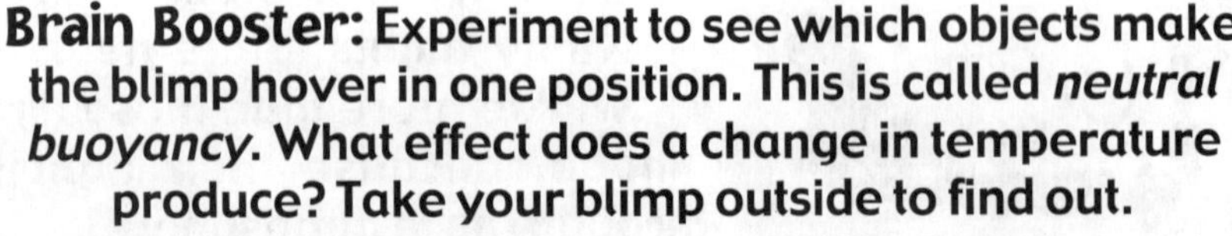

Brain Booster: Experiment to see which objects make the blimp hover in one position. This is called *neutral buoyancy*. What effect does a change in temperature produce? Take your blimp outside to find out.

© Instructional Fair • TS Denison